www.tredition.de

AF197161

Arnold H. Lanz

Top 10 Health

75 years old - and untouched by age

www.tredition.de

Cover, illustration: Arnold H. Lanz
Editing: Arnold H. Lanz
Translation: Viviane Weber

Publisher: tredition GmbH, Hamburg

ISBN
Paperback: 978-3-7482-0610-1
Hardcover: 978-3-7482-0611-8
e-Book: 978-3-7482-0612-5

TOP 10 HEALTH

75 years old - and untouched by age

Content

Preamble

Slowly I'm 75 years old - and feel today much younger, more vital, more articulated and emotionally balanced than 30 to 40 years ago.

Many people are at the age of 50 or at the age of 60 drained and yearn to finally get out of work and retire. I did not only work until I was 65, but I'll be working until 75! Well, I run a health practice and I enjoy it - but work is and remains effort, concentration and commitment, not to say pressure, strain and stress.

So how can I handle that?

Quite simple: I apply the Top 10 Health. I integrated them into my daily life.

Preliminary remark

I consciously represent anatomical connections in a very simple, non-scientific language. This leads to inaccuracies that I accept, and I kindly ask you, dear reader, to forgive me. The big advantage of this procedure is: I can present the most important points of health in a memorable and easily comprehensible way.

If you value medically correct reasons, would like to learn about backgrounds, then I recommend you my book Mr. X, (Mr. Health-X). In this book you will find evidence, explanations, references to studies, etc.

In addition, other topics such as hormone balance, sexuality, psyche, mental power, colors, fragrances, etc. The book also contains dozens of practical examples, recovery courses and details of what has actually led to recovery.

Health Rule # 1: Exercise, Exercise, Exercise!

We humans are motor machines. We are not animals, no, but a comparison cannot harm. What does a fox do all day? Yes, he sleeps a lot - and in the rest of the time, he sweeps around. He walks up to 50 kilometers a day to look for food. Deer, elephants, tigers, lions, elks, wild cats and all the birds, insects, butterflies, mice and fish all live the same life - all the animals move a lot.

Our ancestors did it too. The story of the Aborigines, the Indians, the African primitive peoples - all show the same thing: Hiking, roaming, looking for food.

We do not do all that anymore today. Our life has become more civilized and therefore easier. We buy the food in the shop or restaurant - and use our time for something better.

We drive to work by car or public transport, sit or stand around for hours, make one-sided movements or work almost with our heads and move little or not at all.

Is that smarter?

Perhaps easier, safer and more lucrative too, mostly as well more comfortable, but smarter? No!

Our body has been the same for many thousands of years. Long legs, long arms, little trunk and organs that only work if they get enough exercise.

Organs need movement? Yes, of course! Does digestion say something to you? Peristalsis? Lymph?

Without enough exercise, our entire machinery suffers. It threatens a whole series of diseases and ailments: From heart attack risk to constipation, varicose veins, hemorrhoids, arteriosclerosis and brain calcifications. I do not even list them all, the list is endless, because ultimately almost every illness is due to a lack of blood flow. That's still not all.

Without movement, the lymph, the nutrient and clarifier flow come to a halt. You become increasingly sluggish and sooner or later freeze like Lot's wife.

Don't believe me, go to a retirement home and look at the immobility there. Geriatric doctors see it as "normal" that you become immobile and slower. Me, not at all and I'm soon 75 years old. There is no reason why you cannot remain physically and mentally fit and flexible up to the very highest age. Not one reason. Unless you are not moving - or moving wrong.

In terms of movement, people can be divided into three classes:

	Movement people	Tormentors	Pashas
Character	They explode when they can't move. Competitive sports, walk events, marathons.	They know that exercise is important. They have a bad conscience. When they move, they torment themselves fiercely.	Consciously or unconsciously chosen ideal: Winston Churchill:[1] Why should I walk when I can sit, why should I sit if I can lie down?
Top or Flop	Although they are usually well-trained, fun often	They try to catch up movement and exercise in a	Only the sloth thinks about such a beha-

---

[1] Winston Churchill's constitution of a horse (resistance) copes with his health-endangering lifestyle many years. But in 1955 he suffered a stroke and what came after were only pain.

leads to bloody seriousness and overburdening.	fiercely power explosion. Since they are barely trained, they move quickly in the anaerobic area [2]	vior, unfortunately we humans not.

To put it bluntly: The development requirement for us humans was: A walking machine.

Just like the fox who goes daily, wanders around. Or like the Aborigines, who wander every day. Or like the Indians on the prowl: Go for long distances, crawl, stalk, crouch, ambush, jump up, run short distance and then on the way home: Walk, walk, walk.

Our body machine is built for that.

Yes, I know: Tennis, squash, marathon, football, handball, figure skating; we can do all that, too. But it does not actually belong to the original development goal of the human.

Recommendation

All this is followed by a recommendation that is as simple as it is consistent: To walk, hike and march every day for 30 to 60 minutes.

No, I'm not talking about walking and looking at flowers and butterflies. And no, I'm not talking about breathless sweating on the treadmill.

---

[2] The anaerobic threshold is the stress limit in sports physiology. A regular workout with an intensity just below this threshold is considered very effective in building endurance performance.

I'm talking about at least 30 minutes going out in the fresh air. Marching in one piece, without a break. At the rate at which the breath is regular and deep, the heart beats with a slightly increased frequency, but does not rattle. At a pace that can be adapted to the terrain: Very speedy in the plane, slower uphill, in which you can warm the whole body well, but not break out in sweat.

You are welcome to drive to a beautiful place, into the forest or to a stream and walk there, because it is particularly recreative there. But a journey route is not necessary. You can do this with a lot of enjoyment on Saturday and Sunday. During the week, it is sufficiently to go out the door and walk. Just get out and walk.

Yes, I know you are in stress and have no time for your daily 30 minutes. Good, that's ok. Just do not be surprised if you have your first streak, if you need an artificial knee joint, get diabetes, hay fever, varicose veins, back pain, constipation, and so on.

And if your life expectancy per year immobility drops by a month.

Just calculate it: Your statistical life expectancy is around 75 to 80 years. Every year immobility is a month less. For how many years have you missed the daily 30 minutes march? Just settle it out.

And then consider whether it might not be worthwhile to include 30 minutes in your daily routine. You can march everywhere, e.g. also on the way to work.

Please take care: It has to be in one piece.

Yes, I know, you move a lot at work, make the household, run into the basement.

Is that 30 minutes at a time? No? Then unfortunately it does not do what you want: Life extension.

Yes, of course you can also count on it: Every year regular exercise brings a monthly extension of life.

And I'm not talking about a life with joint pain, beginning Alzheimer's, spasms, hemorrhoids, tinnitus, rheumatism, dentition, hearing aid, etc. No, I'm not interested in such a life. Especially not when it's called poles, walker, wheelchair, hospital bed. Even if millions of people let it down and the doctor talks about age-related degradation; Such a future is not really worth living.

When I speak of life extension, then only as I experience it: 100% painless, vital, articulated and in full possession of my senses.
You can reach that, too. Now think about how to integrate movement into your life and then go to Chapter 2.

Rule # 1: Walk, because hiking is a species-appropriate movement!
We humans are running machines. Tennis, football, climbing etc. in all honors, but our whole body is geared to walking, marching, running. 30 minutes of walking every day is the best guarantee for a long, trouble-free life. Every year regular walking increases the life expectancy by one month.

Health Rule #2: Forget Red Bull!

Red Bull has managed to become the world's most famous sports drink within a few decades. Is it really that good, does it help athletes?
No, just the opposite.
We humans consist of 66% water. I say it consciously again: Water. Not Red Bull, coffee, beer, wine, tea, milk, orange juice!
Just imagine: If you weigh 60 kg, that's 40 kg of water and 20 kg of skin, bones, brain and organic material.

The 40 kg / liter of water contain about 5 liters of blood. The rest, so 35 liters, is water. More precisely, this rest should be water and not red bull, beer, etc.
Where exactly are these 35 liters? A bit everywhere. You could say, primarily in the cell gaps; in the subcutaneous tissue, the organs and in the gastrointestinal tract. What is the water doing there? It supplies the cells with vital substances (nutrient stream) and it cleans the waste, slags, bacteria, viruses, fungi, etc. (clarification stream). The big question is, how does the organism of Red Bull, beer, milk and tea manage to generate a valuable cell nutrient flow? This Herculean task costs the organism an enormous amount of work and sweat and consumes your vitality.
If you are often tired, start to drink water instead of Red Bull and so on. You simplify your organism to fulfill its tasks easier.
The second big question is, how does the water get to the cells and how is the sewage stream moved? By many people you have to ask: Is the sewage stream even moving? Just go to a nursing home. You can see what happens when the sewage stream slumps. You become increasingly immobile, clumsy, stiff, calcified, petrified. Every getting up is only

possible with a lot of groaning, every step causes pain and you wonder if you do not want to stay seated.

The lymph is only moved by contracting and relaxing the muscles. That way we're back to Rule # 1: Movement.

To complete Rule # 2: Your skin is permeable, i.e. you lose one to two liters at night. So, a good advice is: When you get up, you should first drink two to three glasses of pure, lukewarm water. Slow and enjoyable. Depending on the activity, you lose one to three liters of water during the day. Your body needs constantly replenishment. The amount depends on your eating habits. If you eat a lot of vegetables and fruits, then one liter is enough, if you eat starchy carbohydrates (bread, pasta, rice, corn) then it should be three liters or more. The same applies to wine, coffee, beer, orange juice: These are real water robbers.

Drinking, drinking, drinking is the motto. Water, nothing but pure, crystal clear water. Without carbonation please, because acid eats your joints.

Drinking, that is very important, not with meals, but between meals. Why this? When you eat, the stomach begins to produce stomach acid. If you drink now, you water down the acid and your stomach gets stressed. Your digestion works much better if you drink before and after meals, but not during meals.

Rule # 2: Drink, because water is more important than anything else!

For the most part we are made of water, covered with skin, structured by bones and organs. Unfortunately, we lose water, we have to supplement it constantly, renew it. Wine, beer, tea, coffee, red bull, etc. cause many problems for the organism. One to three liters of water, as pure as possible, supplement the supply, ensure the nutrient flow and keep the skin and organs vital.

Health Rule # 3: Avoid Junk Food!

Yes, I know, you have been aware of this for a long time. You try to avoid eating chips, fries, burgers. But wait, I have to take the scope much wider. As junk food I call everything that your organism can not or hardly digest. This makes the list longer, much longer. This includes all E-number products, fortified, refined ready meals such as ready-to-serve pizza, fruit yoghurt, all light products, cereals and cornflakes, margarine, bars, chewing gum etc.
Is that all? No, not at all. The American institute "Nutrition & Healing" has listed which foods are most dangerous to health.

Food product	Occurrence	Disease risk	To be replaced with
Sugar	Soft drinks Pastry Chocolate Ketchup etc.	Fatty liver Acidity Rheumatism, arthritis, polyarthritis, fibromyalgia, MS etc.	Stevia Erythrit
Fruit juices	Orange juice Grapefruit juice Apple juice etc.	Acidity Rheumatism, arthritis, polyarthritis, fibromyalgia, MS etc.	Pure, natural water

Cereals	Cornflakes	Gastrointesti-nal problems Leaky Gut Cancer	Vegetables, fruits
Starchy carbo-hydrates: Wheat Rice Amaranth Quinoa Oatmeal etc.	Bread Pasta Rice Corn Potatoes Sweet potatoes	Diabetes The whole rheumatic dis-order spect-rum Cancer	Fresh vege-table Fresh fruits
Soy	Tofu Soy milk	Hormonal problems Cancer	Vegetables, fruits
Omega 6 ex-cess fats and oils	Olive, rape-seed, sunflo-wer, thistle oil, etc.	All inflamma-tory diseases, especially rheumatism, arthritis	Linseed oil Coconut oil Butter / fried butter Ghee

Maybe I should have listed better what is natural for us humans, what we can digest well. This is actually quite simple, because a good, nutritious, easily digested meal always contains the following ingredients:

Easily digestible, complete meal:

Protein	At each meal a protein, so eggs or fish or pulse (legume) or meat or dairy products
Vegetable and or fruits	Vegetables and fruits can be combined as desired, raw or cooked, e.g. salad with carrots, tomatoes, celery and or ratatouille. The same applies to fruits: Compote / fruit salad
Fat	Coconut fat for frying, linseed oil for salad, dips etc.

Eat three meals daily, preferably at the same times, e.g. at 07.00, 12.00, 18.00. Keep eating breaks for 4 -5 hours. Nothing during the eating break: No chewing gum, coffee, bars, apple – only water.

For your meals to succeed, here is the list of well digestible foods:
- Vegetables such as broccoli, cauliflower, cabbage, tomatoes, savoy cabbage, carrots, celery, etc.
- Fruits such as apple, pear, apricot, melon, grapes, bananas, oranges etc.
- Berries such as strawberries, raspberries, blueberries, currants, etc.
- Herbs and spices such as parsley, chives, thyme, sage, rosemary, basil
- Wild herbs such as dandelion, giersch, ribwort plantain
- Protein such as fish, eggs, veal, beef, chicken, duck, venison, dairy etc.
- Vegetable protein, e.g. peas, lentils, kidney beans, etc.
- Fats and oils: Please limit yourself to linseed (flaxsee) oil, coconut oil, butter, fried butter

Anyone who listens to his body realizes that even from this list he cannot easily digest everything. Some tolerate broccoli better, the other cauliflower. What you personally digest well, you should let analyze.[3] Please look for someone, who also analyzes whether you eat enough, too little, too much protein, fruits, vegetables, carbohydrates, fat. These proportions are individual and the supply of the body with these basic ingredients is very important. Do not get confused by fashion trends like Paleo, food combining, vegetarianism, etc. We humans basically need protein, vegetables, fruits and easily digestible fats. What we do not need or only in very, very small quantities are sugar and starch.

CRP

Second, you should monitor your CRP value, your inflammatory factor. A value of over 50 is in the conventional medicine a limit value to the rheumatic type. With 50 or more you have rheumatism, arthritis, polyarthritis, fibromyalgia, gout. But no doctor has to tell you that, you can feel that very clearly: Joint pain, pain when getting up, pain when walking; every movement feels like hell. You could scream out of pain and nobody will tell you how to get that damn CRP value down, because pain and rheumatism in old age are considered as normal. After all, there are cortisone, painkillers, ointments and the many sinister (rheumatism-) special preparations. If you love disappointments, then try them all out, that will take away your illusions. Finally, only morphine remains. But even that does not numb the pain any more.

---

[3] Food analyzes such as "metabolic typing" is helpful.

Is there really no alternative?

I've heard there are carbon rollators and lightweight wheelchairs. Look stylish, they say. One is allegedly faster with it than with the ordinary ones. But what helps you, if every movement is painful?

Unless you don't stop eating starchy carbs and sugar, the pain will remain.

You can choose. The dear pasta, the oh so crispy bread - or pain-free. It's your choice. Nobody forces you to eat inflammatory foods.

Yes, it takes some discipline and a rethinking to let go and replace all the starch and sugar. But man is a habit animal. Get into your new, sugar-free habits - and you'll see: It's just great! First, you digest fruits and vegetables much easier than pasta, rice, corn, bread, potatoes. And second, the pain gradually disappears. No, not right now. After all, you've stuffed this sugar-paste mass into you for years. Or not?

If you are then painless and fully mobile again, then you can announce your walker for sale by auction. Rheumatism does not come back - unless you don't fall back into old habits.

Do you remember how it was in youth? You've jumped over obstacles, taken two or three steps at a time, hopped carefree, danced, moved lightly and weightlessly. And today: Every step is a torment. And even worse: The strength is missing: You cannot even unscrew an ordinary water bottle.

There's a way back to that youthful agility: Zero sugar, zero starch, and lots and lots of flaxseed oil. You have to detoxify, because you have to drive the consequences of your sugar addiction out of the body. You have to cleanse your sugared, syrup-like, fermenting, stinking clarifier. How, I'll explain you later on. First, remove starch and sugar from your diet and eat a lot, yes, much more vegetables, fruits and berries.

Rule # 3: Attention Food: Eat only what you can digest!

Eating is easy, but always remember: Everything you put in your mouth has to work on your organs. If they fail to digest, diarrhea results or the body must form a depot. And there, right there, your health problems start.

Diseases may have different fathers, but they always have only one mother: Food that your body can not digest.

Health Rule # 4: Full fat

I'll ask you directly: Are you fat? I know, such a question is indecent - but you do not want to be decent first, but healthy.

On the subject weight or overweight, there is actually a reliable statement, the BMI (Body Mass Index).

For many people, but mostly for women, that's not the point. I have seen many who, according to the BMI, were well within the norm, but nevertheless felt unwell and fat and desperately wanted to lose weight. The thought of the thin model haunts around in many minds. Full fat, this manipulation of a healthy feeling, right?

Anyway, let's take care of the fats, because most people think they get fat from fat. That's where the whole greasy problem starts.

Most of my new patients tell me that they eat healthily. If I then ask what is healthy then one of the first answers is: "I eat as little fat as possible".

Good or wrong?

Wrong! For exactly two reasons:

- The little amount of fat you eat is not digestible, unhealthy fat (if it were not, you would not gain weight).
- And second, because you eat too little fat, you have too little energy to lose weight. Losing weight is an additional task of the organism. He does it reliably, as long as he has enough energy for it.

Yes, I know, the subject of fat is not easy. Is there not LDL and HDL, good and bad fats, trans fats, short chain and long chain, cholesterol etc.?

I can calm you down. All this is not important. It is a cleverly constructed mess of the pharmaceutical lobby to lead as many people as possible into a tablet addiction. [4]

Just among us: Your brain needs amounts of cholesterol. Please keep your memory and common sense and do not swallow any cholesterol counterparts.

For your health there is a simpler, much easier way to classify the type of fats: Their digestibility or their effect on your health. Let me explain this a little bit more:
Any form of oil and fat, including fat in nuts, avocado, meat, milk, cheese, etc. is always a mixture of different omega fatty acids. The fatty acids are divided into omega 3, 5, 6, 7, 9. What do you need to know?

---

[4] Cholesterol - the big bluff:
On November 30, 2017 TV channel *Arte* broadcasted a documentary about cholesterol. It documents the onset of the claim that cholesterol reduces the risk of heart attack, and then follows all the steps taken by the pharmaceutical lobby to uphold that claim over decades. The measures of the pharma lobby are factually documented in the film It shows how manufacturers are frightening, how brazenly claims are, being made about how blatantly manipulated reports and studies have been. How skillfully constructed scientific theories of good and bad cholesterol, LDL and HDL.
At the end of the film, the situation of today is shown: Millions and millions of people swallow cholesterol-lowering medicine - and the rate of cardiovascular deaths today is exactly the same as 60 years ago. All the people who swallow cholesterol tablets today are nothing more than guinea pigs who volunteer to pay for side effects. No, you do not die directly from cholesterol lowering medicine, but gradually you lose your healthy judgment.
Cardiovascular risks today - like 60 years ago - are still caused by smoking, a lack of exercise, and sugar. Please watch the movie on Youtube: https://www.y-outube.com/watch?v=C6SVB99mJHA

- The fatty acids 5, 7, 9 are unproblematic, your body can deal with it well.
- Omega 6 is a corrosive acid. It causes severe inflammation.
- Omega 3 is the counterpart of Omega 6. Omega 3 balances Omega 6 acidity. Both acids (omega 3 and 6) should therefore be present in our diet in equal parts, so that it does not come to inflammation.
- Unfortunately, our "normal" diet contains far too much omega 6 and hardly ever omega 3 fat. And that's how it comes about: 60 - 80% of all people in Europe, Amercia, Australia suffer from joint pain, muscle pain, rheumatism, arthritis, arthrosis, etc.

So, you can imagine this:
- Omega 3 "lubricates", so it also retains fatty acid, the "greasy" elasticity, the moistening, the nourishing.
- Omega 6 is an acid in the sense of the word: It attacks tissue and even eats away bones.

You should, logically, eat the same amount of Omega 3 as 6, so that no damage occurs in your body.
Do you do that?
In Germany, the omega 3: 6 ratio is recorded statistically. The average of all Germans is 1 : 25. Each German has 25 times more Omega 6 fatty acids in his tissue, his muscles, bones, cartilage, veins stored as omega 3.
Is the ratio in Switzerland, Austria, Belgium, France, Italy, Spain, Great Britain, the United States, Australia etc. better? No, the omega 6 bad habit is rampant almost everywhere. [5]

---

[5] The traditional Japanese cuisine with lots of raw fish is very omega 3 rich.
The Omega 3 : 6 average in Japan was 1: 3 for decades; rheumatic complaints

Over the years, the Omega 6 continues to accumulate and reaches values of 1 : 35, 1 : 50 or even higher from an age of 35 to 50 years. No wonder, then it comes to age-related rheumatism, fibromyalgia, arthritis, polyarthritis.

How old are you today? You can easily estimate where your value is about.

What can you do? You need Omega 3 in rough amounts. Good omega 3 suppliers are:

- Linseed oil (Flax oil)
- Chia seeds, Chia oil
- Sacha Inchi oil
- Fish
- Fish oil, krill oil

Neutral fat oils (equal to omega 3 as 6) are:

- Butter and frying butter
- Coconut oil

You can take Omega 3 in the form of fish / krill oil - but it makes less sense in using Omega 6 (olive, rape, etc.) oil. You never come up with an omega 3 surplus. Reconvert your kitchen. For frying please add butter or coconut oil - for salad, muesli, dips linseed oil. Please do not use any other fats and oils anymore.

How long does the omega conversion take in your body? Years. Bones, cartilage etc. renew in monthes / years.

----

were virtually unknown in Japan.

Is linseed oil indeed useful? Have you ever heard of Johanna Budwig? [6] She has cured cancer patients and indeed the hopeless cases. What did she do for these patients? The Budwig muesli. Main ingredient in it is linseed oil. She recommended 40 to 50 g daily!

So, if you are looking for something that prevents and eliminates rheumatism and co and at the same time avoids cancer, then you have found it here: Linseed oil. Now you have the choice: Believe in advertising about the oh-so-healthy olive oil and keep your pain, or consistently change your fats. You do not have to do it for me, I had polyarthritis and I screamed in pain. I know how horrible that is. But I also learned how linseed oil dissolved all these inflammations. I have been completely free of pain for a long time.

In my experience, you need 2 - 3 tablespoons of linseed oil daily. You can just take it like that. Or would you like to know how I integrated linseed oil into my diet? In a muesli. It is a great alternative to the bread breakfast and bread dinner. I take:

- 200 – 250 g lean curd cheese or cottage cheese or nature yoghurt,
- 2 - 3 tablespoons of linseed oil (20 - 30 g). Stir in linseed oil in the lean curd cheese until it has completely disappeared,
- 250 – 350 g fresh berries or fruits and/or,
- 40 – 60 g dried berries and fruits,
- sprinkle some cinnamon and/or turmeric over it, stir in,
- on request, 1 small teaspoon of honey or agave syrup or stevia, xylitol or bee pollen.

This results in a meal of around 400 calories.

---

[6] Johanna Budwig, 30.09.1908 – 19.05.2003, German pharmacist and biochemist, she healed patients with her linseed-oil – protein food.

PS 1: I almost forgot, there is still the subject of overweight.
Obesity is always caused by the following factors:

- Wrong fats or a wrong omega 3 : 6 ratio,
- Sugar, starch-containing foods,
- Digestive organs that are not really powerful,
- Low energy level: The organism cannot generate enough energy from food.

PS 2: Another word on cholesterol, because on cholesterol abstruse information exist, as it is purely natural and an important body's substance. What do you think, where do you have the most cholesterol? Cholesterol is present throughout the body, but in the brains we have the highest concentration. As a toddler, we begin to learn, in school and in education this continues. Even as a child, we "enlarge" our brains continuously and thus the amount of cholesterol increases. Later, in professional life with further education, news, learning foreign languages, newspapers, television, holiday experiences, etc. that goes on and on. We stuff information into our brains for a lifetime and expect it to constantly adapt and grow. As a rule, it does this without a problem - as long the cholesterol mass increases.

Who in the world came up with the crazy idea of lowering cholesterol? Do they want us to go gaga, to lose the memories and the memory?
You can choose: Cholesterol-lowering medicine or a vital, powerful memory - until death.

Rule # 4: Consistently only eat digestible fats!
The topic of fat and oils is quite simple. You can digest butter, fried butter, coconut oil and linseed oil. Linseed oil loses its Omega 3 content when you heat it up. Take fried butter or coconut oil for frying and for everything else linseed oil. These fats you can digest well and they do not make you fat.

Health Rule # 5: Do not be like Lot's wife!

Lot was led out of the sinful city of Sodom by angels, but Lot's wife turned and froze to the pillar of salt. Is this also today?
Yes!
The physicians call it osteoarthritis: Calcified, fossilized joints. Or arteriosclerosis, brain calcification (vascular calcification). Stroke, dementia, Alzheimer's etc. are not far away.
Where does all this lime, all this calcium come from?
Calcium is abundant in food and usually in water. In itself, this is not a problem for our organism. If he has enough trace elements available, he can easily dispose of the surplus.
If he has insufficient amounts of boron, D3, K2, magnesium, he cannot do that. Then he begins to invest deposits, i.e. it deposits lime in arteries, in the shoulder, the knuckles, the brain, etc.
If you have joint pain or even beginning deformations, then you can still listen to the gibberish about "wear and tear" and "age" or you become active and help your body get rid of the lime stiffeners.

You only have these two options. If you believe the gibberish, then you have already lost. Then you should immediately seek someone who will help you, care for you, push your wheelchair.
On the other hand, if you do not believe the stupid gossip, but trust in the self-healing powers of your organism and strongly support them, then you can remain agile, and vital to the highest age. I'll show you how it works.
How do you clean your bathroom, your kitchen? I mean, how do you remove lime? With vinegar or lemon, right? Exactly the same applies to your lime deposits. Recipes can be found in Attachment # 2.

Dismantling the existing deposits is the one thing. The other is to stop or reverse the ever-increasing deposit in your joints and arteries. What do you need for this? I said it already: Boron, D, K, magnesium or- in one word: Minerals and trace elements. And this in rough quantities.

Boron is probably the least known substance, so here's the list of what boron does: Boron

- builds up bones (helps the organism to use calcium properly),
- breaks down pathological calcifications in tissue, in organs, in joints (reverses arterial calcification!),
- helps to heal fractures quickly,
- harmonizes the hormone balance,
- improves cell membrane function (and thus has a positive effect on Alzheimer's, cancer).

Rule # 5: Avoid calcification, because lethally quiet trickles the calcification!

According to statistics, 80 to 90% of all elderly people suffer from calcification in some form. You have the best chance of being petrified like Lot's wife. Today, this does not happen suddenly, but much more "comfortable" on poles, walker, wheelchair, hospital bed. But it is still associated with hellish pain.

This is the future you will have when you are not getting active and helping your body wash out calcification and stop new deposits. Take lemon, apple vinegar, boron, K2, D3, magnesium! And move - daily!

Health Rule # 6: Use Green Power!

We live in an environment that is anything but healthy. Our organs are exposed to a variety of burdens, as the list in Attachment # 3 shows. For that reason alone, detoxification, deacidification, deslagification are life-long tasks.

How bad are the burdens on our organism, we learn only fragmented. The late effects of the diverse and still increasing radiation exposure, for example, are only vaguely known. One suspects that this will not go well, but since we all no longer want to do without mobile phones, computers, photovoltaics, TGV, ICE (high-speed trains) etc., we do not want to know it exactly.

Does this attitude help our organism? No, not at all. He is in the middle of it and needs to expand it. How can we detoxify our system, protect against these multiple environmental influences? Well, fire is best dealt with by fire. Environmental influences, environmental damage thus with primeval environmental force. Where do we find them? In the green power.

Surely you know Spirulina and Chlorella. They are recommended for metal and heavy metal contamination. Do they also help against the cocktail of polluting substances brought to us by the spray agent manufacturers, the chemical industry, food manufacturers, cell phone operators, etc.?

Yes, greenery is the most effective environmental damage diversion.

Would you like to know how I got rid of my chronic fatigue, the nervous breakdown, my latent burnout, the multiple pains, the ubiquitous nipples, in short, all of my environmental damage? And how I constantly protect myself from all the environmental smog? I make smoothies. I pack in as much invigorating and detoxifying sun power as possible.

My smoothies are as follows:

- First, I give pure water or vegetable juice or very diluted fruit juice in the high-performance mixer, it is supposed to become a drink. Then I add:
- Fresh (wild) plants such as dandelion, ribwort, giersch, melissa, basil, parsley, chives,
- Detoxifying plants such as thyme, oregano, sage, mint (fresh or dried),
- A heaped spoon of green plants concentrate with chlorella, spirulina, wheat grass, barley grass, white tea, green tea, alfalfa, turmeric, garlic, ginger, goji, acai. The concentrate powder also contains adaptogens, so eleuthero, rhodiola, ashwagandha, ginseng etc., as well as mushrooms such as maitake, cordyceps, reishi, shitake, agaricus,
- I will then give, for the taste and according to the mood: Bananas, apricots, watermelons, cucumbers, spinach, lettuce or cabbage leaves, etc. I make sure that I am not only adding berries and fruits, but always add plenty green vegetables as well,
- And at the end I add one tablespoon of linseed oil.

Yes, I hear the sigh: "Oh my gosh, complicated." Just make it easy: Find a green-power powder that contains a most complete mixture: Different grasses, wild plants, green tea, alfalfa, mushrooms, spices, adaptogens, etc. This powder you can supplement with herbs from the garden, with green vegetables and fruits.

Yes, you can also just buy wheatgrass or chlorella. Then you have a simple, small bag knife. That's it, that's how you get flat on shrews. Unfortunately, the environmental burdens are not cute mice, they are adult tigers, lions, hyenas. So, use the full, concentrated green-power power.

Rule # 6: Use the full power of Green Power!
We live in a very interesting time - which unfortunately holds loads of burdensome environmental influences and environmental toxins. Fire is best combated with (contra-) fire, environmental toxins with environmental-natural-primal force. Prepare daily a green-power smoothie in which you mix in as much nature detoxification power as you can.

Health Rule # 7: Fight the Battle of the Righteous!

Detoxification, as we saw it, is an ongoing task because our environment is burdened.

Do we have other things that burden our normal life, hamper, disturb, shorten - things that make us sick? Unfortunately, yes. And what kind of! We human beings are the most highly developed form of life, correspondingly large is the thrust that wants to profit in some way. Yes, I'm talking about viruses, bacteria, parasites, worms, fungi, prions.

If someone puts you in the public transport, then you get a fat load of these pathogens, and your risk to come down with these is correspondingly high. But these germs are not only then around you, but always. They are ubiquitous in the truest sense of the word.

Do you have a fruit bowl at home? Have you ever wondered where all the little flies come from?

Yesterday there was nothing and today there are hundreds. Yesterday all fruits were still intact, today it has foul spots.

Did you put leftovers in the fridge and wonder a few days later that they had mold?

It's just like that, we're surrounded by fungi, viruses, bacteria, parasites. There are few things that are long lasting, that are not attacked, that do not bum: Pasta, cornflakes, sugar. The meaning of the matter is, if even the whole armada of decomposition bacteria cannot get rid of the cereals, pasta, etc., how should our digestive tract manage?

Impossible.

So stop eating them. That's what we saw in Rule # 3.

Here we have to think about how to cope with viruses, bacteria, etc. What do I hear, you have none? But still several times a year sinusitis, bladder inflammation, flu, rash, tinnitus, diarrhea, constipation, swollen legs, runny nose, menstruation pain, herpes, aphtha, etc.?

What do you think, where does this come from?

It does not come from the Internet, that's for sure. They are tangible bacilli and they are in you. And, unfortunately, not positive at all. On the contrary, they carry one attack after another, because they want to live, multiply. At your expense.

Whether you like it or not, you have to go against it. Otherwise they will eat you up, sooner or later. The galling begins with flu and ends with MS, Crohn's disease, Alzheimer's, hay fever, cancer, autoimmune disease.

So you do well to keep your house as clean as possible. Start cleaning it today.

How does conventional medicine work? She uses antibiotics, often unfortunately only when it is already burning. Does that help? Ostensibly often yes. Does it eliminate the pathogens? Usually incomplete, because antibiotics are effective against bacteria, but not against viruses, fungi, prions, parasites. It takes more against that.

It needs living, vital substances that cope with the unfortunately also very lively and adaptable pathogens.

Be aware: Antibiotics is a rigid, chemical formula. It works only as long as the pathogen is not mutated. He mutates, he is alive.

So you need something that keeps up with the mutations. And you can find that in the plant world. Plants are subject to the same environmental conditions as bacilli, they keep up.

But which plant, how processed, how dosed? There begins the great art.

Herbal antibiotics: Essential oils

Thyme, oregano, cloves, rosemary, grapefruit seed extract, juniper, myrrh, mint, cinnamon and many other plants have a wonderfully broad spectrum of activity: Antiviral, antiparasitic, antimucoid, antibacterial. Exactly what we want: They work against viruses, parasites, fungi, bacteria, priones.

The highest concentration of plant compounds is found in the essential oils.

Highly concentrated ammunition against everything that threatens, strains, and shortens human life. In France, mixtures of essential oils against flu, otitis media, parasite infestation, sinusitis, herpes, helicobacter, etc. are offered. These mixtures have the great advantage that on the one hand they act considerably broader than antibiotics and on the other hand have no side effects. In addition, they are relatively cheap.

So if you have some chronic suffers, find a specialist who will make you a mix.

If you do not know your exact illness, then this recipe will help: [7]

mg	Latin	English
05	Carum carvi	Caraway
10	Juniperus communis	Common juniper
25	Rosmarinus ABV	Rosemary
10	Mentha piperita	Peppermint
05	Laurus nobilis	Bay
20	Anethum graveolens	Dill
25	Ocimum basilicum	Basil

---

[7] Composition HES Purifiant HE of the Pharmacie des Eaux Vives in Geneva.

How important is the war against germs?

According to estimates, 80 to 90% of all people are burdened with helicobacter bacteria. About 50 to 60% carry cytomegalovirus, Epsteinbarr, herpes, influenza, adeno viruses around. And the mush-rooms and parasites do not look any better. Except fatigue, occasional discomfort, you hardly feel it; that is normal. The pathogens do not want to be recognized, otherwise you will be active, go to the doctor and get antibiotics. Even parasites are not necessarily "felt" in everyday life. Amoebae, liver flukes, worms can drive their mischief unnoticed for a long time. Nevertheless, they are an enormous burden for your organism. Among other things, they ensure that the superacid climate in your body remains nicely toxic-acidic. And they prepare, quietly and uncannily, diseases such as hay fever, MS, leaky gut, asthma, autoimmune diseases and, above all, cancer.

Of course, you can continue to be ignorant, hospitable, and tolerate all the kinking, and sincerely hope that it does not hit you, that all the pathogens will not make your life hell. Do not be angry with me, but I cannot give you a guarantee; None, not even for the next month.

And I cannot fight for you either. You have to do that yourself. [8]

Go to the specialist, to the specialized pharmacy, call in Geneva.

The sooner you start to fight, the sooner you are rid of the crowd.

And if you think you're rid of your burdens, remember: 60 - 90% of all people around you have aggressive microbes in them. The bad guys are never far away from you. You do well to always take essential oils.

---

[8] In my practice, I also use special homeopathy against detected viruses, parasites, prions, etc. This method increases the effectiveness but requires an individual analysis and therefore cannot be presented here.

If you are free of your chronic diseases for months, have no more pain, can jump as in your youth, then a number smaller is sufficient, then it must not be the whole recipe of the Geneva pharmacy. For daily cleaning there are e.g. tablets with oregano oil, ginger, fennel.

Yes, I can see it: You doubt and think: Is it really like this, are there always pathogens around us? I'll give you an example: Do you know mosquitoes? I mean those little, annoying things. They weigh no 2 g, are fragile and lottery-shaped, but they have a highly effective sting. Penetrate through your skin until they find your blood vessels. Is that not incredible? These little, puny things and so aggressive?

I'm sure you do not attract mosquitoes specifically and when they are there, you want to scare them away. Is that useful? No. The mosquitoes are naturally and aggressive and they sting.

In Europe Mosquitoes are comparatively harmless. Ticks are much lousier. I saw many patients with years of paralysis. Only the massive use of essential oils did eliminate the issue of the problem.

Unfortunately, there are not only visible and perceptible attackers such as mosquitoes and ticks. Insidious are all the viruses, bacteria, parasites, which we do not necessarily feel immediately. But even if we do not (immediately) feel it, believe me, they are omnipresent, treacherous, aggressive and know only one thing: Their own survival. And that means for you stress, disability, pain, illness and even cancer.

You are good at defending yourself. Get essential oils.

Rule # 7: Use Essential Oils!

Believe me, there are pathogens behind every illness, really behind every illness. This applies to flu as well as rash, open legs, migraine, rheumatism, asthma, cardiovascular problems, MS, Parkinson's, cancer etc. etc.

The most effective weapon we have against it are essential oils. Only they combat reliably viruses, fungi, parasites, bacteria, prions. They have the great advantage that they cause no side effects and are also relatively cheap.

Health Rule # 8: Free Your Organs!

Are essential oils sufficient to stay healthy?

Well, they help you and your organs to get rid of the most burdensome burdens. But it's like in your apartment. There is dust next to dirt. The sky knows where it comes from, but it is there, delivered every day, free and free house. That's the fact.

The organs suffer from it. It's like they do not get enough air to breathe, they slow down, they just work hard.

The question remains: How can you get rid of this daily layer of dust?

Who keeps you healthy? The immune system? Yes, with the help of the organs. They secure the life functions. The heart sets the pace, the lungs provide the organs with oxygen, the gastrointestinal supplies them with vital substances, the liver helps to digest and detoxify, the kidneys regulate the water balance, etc.

Modern medicine pretends that you can replace organs, joints, etc. Do not fool yourself, many patients came to me after bile surgery, liver transplantation, after an artificial joint, they had a lot of pain and problems.

You do well to care of your organs.

It would be nice if you could take them out, clean them, oil them. Sorry, now I've slipped into medical thinking.

Removing and cleaning is not necessary at all. And replacing - with a few exceptions – neither nor.

My father and my mother, both, died of heart issues. I have inherited a double cardiovascular weakness - and then I fainted twice, fell down and only woken up in the hospital after caring. My heart had dropouts, my blood pressure was very low, it seemed like my pump was not pumping properly at all. Do I have a pacemaker? Did I die early?

No. I cared for my heart.

Does it work?

Surely! You can take care of the organs, free them from the constant layer of dust.

You think you have no such burden? This really makes me wonder: Tell me, how do you do that, that no dust falls on you, that not everything is dusted?

And another question:

Did you inhale chamomile, lime blossom, sage, thyme in your last ear nose and throat troubles or did you take any chemicals?

Did you drink a tea or a mother tincture mix with fennel, caraway, lady's mantle, pansy, or did you take any chemicals when you had gastrointestinal problems?

What are you using? Chemistry or plant power?

I mean, what do you do with constipation, gastrointestinal problems, colds, chronic coughing, kidney pain, headache, tinnitus, asthma, joint pain, skin rash?

How long ago was it that you used herbal, natural remedies?

Months? Years?

Then the dust layer on your organs is probably several centimeters thick. Or there is already a thorny scrub like in Sleeping Beauty.

Functional weaknesses of the organs, pain is best countered by plant power: Mother tincture drops, plant tablets / herbal mixtures, spagyric, tea. The effects of herbs have been researched for millennia, there are probably no other means that have been questioned as varied as plants. So use it. Here are some examples of proven plant blends:* [9]

---

[9] Own recipes and recipes of P. Brechbühl, drugstore, Sigriswil and L. Hutter, non-medical practitioner, St. Gallen, both in Switzerland

Gastrointestinal Mother tincture mixture	Liver-Gall Mother tincture mixture	Care of the respiratory system Mother tincture mixture	Cardiovascula Mother tincture mixture
Mentae	Taraxacum	Equisetum	Crataegus
Millefoli	Cynara scol.	Petasites	Leonurus
Melissae	Centauri	Tropaeolum	Melissae
Absinthum	Menthae	Chamomilla	Passiflora
Matricariae	Carvi	Primula	Avena Sativa
Centauri		Thymus	Cactus grandiflor
Carvi aethero-leum		Lycopus	
Rosmarini			

Kidney Mixed herbs	Joint Cartilage, bones Mixed herbs*	Adrenal Endocrine system Mixed herbs	Nerves Mixed herbs
Cranberry	Equisetum arvense	Eleutjerococ-cus	Avena sativa
Burdock, lab herb	Plantago major	Ginseng	Lanvendula
Corn Silk, Corn	Ulmus rubra	Ashwagandha	Cinnamon
Dandelion	Arctium lappa	Rhodolia	Eleutherococcus
Tumeric	Tumeric		Hypericum
	Comniphora Molmol		Melissae
			Passiflora
			Petasites

* depending on the situation, to be supplemented with minerals (boron, K2, calcium, magnesium, manganese, zinc), vitamins C and E as well as collagen and glucosamines.

Rule # 8: Free and regenerate your organs!
Plant mixtures help the organs to get rid of pollution. Plant power is the most efficient regeneration aid. If you want to avoid or get rid of countersinks, blockers, thinners etc., then take care of your organs. Help them to regenerate with herbal blends and you will experience true, real wonders.

Health Rule # 9: Use vital substances!

I gave many seminars and speeches and was well documented with studies, statistics, laboratory analyzes. I have demonstrated conclusively and clearly that what we can buy today for food is only a shadow of what it used to be.

Yes, I am talking about the nutritional value, the content of vitamins and minerals. Today's fruits and vegetables are conceivable nutritionally poor.

Did people believe and act in getting vitamin tablets? A few maybe, but most shrugged the shoulders and went home.

I felt like the caller in the desert - and finally gave it up.

It was clearly an issue that did interest nobody or people believed in advertising: Vitamins are not necessary and if so, please be careful, overdoses are imminent.

What do statistics say? Do diseases decrease, are all people healthy and happy?

Nope. The opposite is true: The number of diabetes, dementia, cancer, cardiovascular and rheumatic patients has increased massively over the past 30 years.

This fact was the reason why I started with speeches. Even today, I'm still a bit worried that people just do not want to hear that they are voluntarily running into illnesses that they could easily avoid.

What do I hear, you are not like that?

So far so good: Hand on heart: Who is that when climbing stairs? Do you still take light-footed and swinging two steps at once as in your youth or are you out of breath after a few steps?

Out of breath means: Your heart is trying to do a peak, but it cannot. It does not have the necessary gas. Your heart is a muscle. Every muscle needs minerals, especially magnesium. How many bananas do you eat daily? Your heart needs, roughly estimated, 3 bananas per day - and then you have only supplied your heart, but you also have arm muscles, calves, etc. right?

I do not want to paint the devil on the wall, but if you get so quickly out of breath: What happens if the heart cannot do more? Death is not far off then. Then it says: The fun is over.

Do you still think you do not need vitamins?

On one point you are right: You do not need synthetically produced vitamins. Your organism hardly recognizes them, he cannot use them, he has to dispose them with difficulty. They are counterproductive or even dangerous.

But vitamins, minerals and trace elements based on fruits, vegetables, wild berries, etc. concentrates, you definitely need. This in rough quantities. They are not dangerous at all, because you eat fruits, vegetables, grasses, mushrooms, berries, wild herbs, medicinal herbs, etc., only things that your organism knows and can handle easily.

This type of dietary supplement is little known in Europe and barely available, in the US manufacturers over-offer themselves: The one has a product based on 12 natural substances, the next has 30, the next 50, etc.

And, do you still think vitamins and minerals are not important?

Ok, I'll give you another example:

Have you ever tried to connect your 220 Volt hair dryer to a 110 Volt outlet? How much warm air did you get there? A small, gentle breeze at most.

Your dryer requires 220 volts to really blow strong and hot.

That's exactly how your organs are. You need natural nutrients to work actively and vigorously.

Well, did I convince you?

If not, then close the book. You are welcome to stay in your sufferings and ailments - fortunately I do not have to carry them - you alone have the pain and problems. Fortunately, I have overcome my own for years. The decision is yours. I can only list what you need to get well. You have to get healthy yourself.

You want to start concretely? Great, good, ok, that makes me happy. I'll show you how I freed my organs and helped them to recover.

a) Multivitamin

I took (and take daily) a super multivitamin, multimineral. At the beginning, I took three times the recommended amount to fill up my empty vital substance depots. Over time, I have tried many multivitamins, my recommendations can be found in the attachments. The multi-vitamin ensures the basic care of the organs.

b) Constipation

Back then I was overweight and chronically clogged, and I knew that I was going on a detox journey and that the organism had to rely on regular excretion. I changed my diet and also took Colon Cleanse Green, which was dosed so high that I could go to the bathroom at least once a day. My organism needed months to normalize the bowel movement

- fortunately, it works now for decades without any problems and support. Through the change in diet and bowel movement control, I also continuously lost 4 - 5 kg per month. I keep my ideal weight for decades without any problems.

c) Main topic, vulnerability

I had cardiac arrhythmias and hemorrhoids. I have analyzed which pathogens cause these problems and found viruses and fungi. I've had antiviral and antimuscoid essential oils mixed and taken for months. At the same time I bought mother tincture drops for the cardiovascular and venous insufficiency and took these as well.

It takes about three years for my organism to completely regenerate the cardiovascular issue. In all this time I took cardiovascular drops. The regeneration went in stages. The hemorrhoids do not itch anymore, but they broke up at irregular intervals and bled. Every time I bled, I took for another month essential oils. I took the mother tincture drops the whole three years uninterrupted. The bleeding was lost over time and stopped completely. My heartbeat became regular, my severe upper arm pain disappeared and today I am - with soon 75 years - regularly demanding mountain tours. My heart does that with ease. I support it with cardiovascular drops two to three times a year.

d) Cleaning plan

Since everything in our body is related to everything, it is important to care for all organs. In addition to multivitamin, colon cleanse green and cardiovascular, I have taken herbal mixtures or mother tincture drops according to the following plan:

Cleaning plan

Month 1	Gastrointestinal
Month 2	Liver-Gall
Month 3	Cardiovascular (I skipped it since I was constantly supporting the cardiovascular system)
Month 4	Respiratory system
Month 5	Kidney-Bladder
Month 6	Spleen, blood system
Month 7	Lymphatic System
Month 8	Hormone system, hormone producing organs
Month 9	Nervous system
Month 10	Joints, tendons, ligaments

After the tenth month, I started again with gastrointestinal drops. During the second "run" I stayed in the topic of respiratory system for three months because I had a certain sinusitis sensitivity. I have adapted the plan to the identified weaknesses.

e) Acid base, green power

Of course, I also deacidified during the diet change. Over time, I also added green smoothies to my diet. Everything that I present to you here in the book, I have worked out over time, with me and with thousands of patients tested. I was allowed to witness

- how years of joint pain gradually disappeared,
- how headaches, migraines disappeared and never appeared again,
- how tormenting hay fever simply stayed away,
- how chronic bladder-kidney infections disappeared,
- how the menstrual pain resettled,
- like monthly menstrual pains just disappeared,

- how the desire for children, after unsuccessful hormone treatment and artificial insemination, has naturally been fulfilled in a natural way,
- how infertility has been transformed into procreative power,
- like skin rash, open legs disappeared,
- how varices regressed, vein pain disappeared,
- how swollen legs regenerated,
- how chronic cough, asthma just stayed away,
- how sinkers, blockers, thinners could be swapped out and the organs functioned normally again,
- how polyps and cancer were dissolved,
- how depression turned into joy of life,
- how psychotropic drugs became redundant,
- how the menopause was overcome without riots,
- how chronic fatigue has been transformed into vitality,
- how hair loss stopped, brittle nails were regenerated,
- how insomnia turned into soothing refreshing sleep,
- how age spots gradually faded and disappeared,
- how sweaty hands, hot soles disappeared,
- how cold hands, cold feet were well supplied with blood and got warm,
- how seborrheic eczema, aphthae, warts, herpes, shingles, etc. simply disappeared,
- how imminent tooth loss has been stopped,
- how hot flushes did not occur,
- how bedwetting ceased,
- how circular round hair loss stopped and hair regrow naturally,
- how swollen legs and ankles ebbed away and became painless,
- etc., etc.

I think that in my years of practice, I have seen every conceivable disease and suffers. With every patient, I've always done the same thing: Deacidify, detoxify, remove dust – re-establish the organs, support, offer help for regeneration, vital substances, vital substances, vital substances.

What do I hear? Do I have to do this for a lifetime?

Counter question: How is that with you with the house dust? Has the delivery stopped or is it still falling?

Rule # 9: Use vital substances!

Healthy, powerful organs need vitamins, minerals, trace elements in harsh quantities. Analgesia, health and vitality up to the highest age is easily possible. Your organs will work as smoothly as you clean, care for, and give them enough natural vitality nutrients.

Health Rule # 10: Agility on all levels

What do you think, how many joints do you have? 30, 50, 80? I mean, how many potential pain points are in your body?

We humans have something over 200 bones and thus also joints. They are all endowed with sensitive periosteum, cartilage. Keeping it supple and fully functional at all times is a Herculean task for your organism.

Have you ever watched a cat get up? She hooks her fore paws in somewhere and then she stretches her front legs long and at length. Then she does the same for the hind legs. Then she pushes her paws together and makes a big hump. Then she yawns thoroughly. Then she starts running: Cat-like supple and makes "meow". So to speak to you: Well, did you get it?

Would that not be something for you, too? To put the body, muscles, tendons, ligaments into operation? Make sure they are supplied with blood. Feel into the body where it hurts right now?

And now the question for you: How do you get up? How do you put your body into operation?

I tell you how I do it: I do the Five Tibetans every day.

These simple and effective Yoga exercises go back to the very practical monks in the Himalayas.[10] Developed and practiced for many centuries

---

[10] I gave many seminars and then wrote a practical book with detailed instructions: Arnold H. Lanz, Fitness and Relaxation with the Five Tibetans, Scherz Verlag, ISBN 978-3-502-25016-6. Unfortunately there is no english translation. The english original book was written by Peter Kelder. It is free in internet: http://lib.ru/URIKOVA/KELDER/Ancient_Secret_of_the_Fountain_of_Youth-Peter_Kelder.pdf

by people who were on the one hand esoteric-spiritual-wholistic-nature-oriented and on the other hand were in a hard struggle for survival. The Five Tibetans gave them the strength and suppleness to get through the hard day's work, physically, mentally and psychologically.

Well, would that not be something for you? A program that helps you to endure your given life situation, all your hardships, as playfully as easily. Successful, so to speak, with a smile on your face.
Yes, I know you do not have time.
Not even 10 minutes a day?
Think about it. When the pains and ailments are here, you can easily spend hours or days in doctors' waiting rooms or in the hospital. In contrast, 10 minutes a day are a breeze.

So, now I have explained you the 10 most important health rules. Now it's your turn. Start implementing today. I wish you good luck - and good health!

Rule # 10: Stay physically and mentally mobile!
Fitness is on everyone's lips. Most people understand this as only physical-athletic fitness. But it's about much more: Mental health. You can achieve this with a program that is as simple as it is effective: The Five Tibetans. They strengthen your immune system, keep you young, fit, physically and mentally alive.

Then 10 Rules:

Rule # 1: Walk, because hiking is a species-appropriate movement!

We humans are running machines. Tennis, football, climbing etc. in all honors, but our whole body is geared to walking, marching, running. 30 minutes of walking every day is the best guarantee for a long, trouble-free life. Every year, regular walking increases the life expectancy by one month.

My implementation:

_____

_____

_____

_____

_____

_____

_____

_____

_____

_____

_____

_____

_____

Rule # 2: Drink, because water is more important than anything else!

For the most part we are made of water, covered with skin, structured by bones and organs. Unfortunately, we lose water, we have to supplement it constantly, renew it. Wine, beer, tea, coffee, red bull, etc. cause many problems for the organism. One to three liters of water, as pure as possible, supplement the supply, ensure the nutrient flow and keep the skin and organs vital.

My Implementation:

Rule # 3: Attention Food: Eat only what you can digest!

Eating is easy, but always remember: Everything you put in your mouth has to work on your organs. If they fail to digest, diarrhea results or the body must form a depot. And there, right there, your health problems start.

Diseases may have different fathers, but they always have only one mother: Food that your body can not digest.

My Implementation:

_____

_____

_____

_____

_____

_____

_____

_____

_____

_____

_____

_____

Rule # 4: Consistently only eat digestible fats!

The topic of fat and oils is quite simple. You can digest butter, fried butter, coconut oil and linseed oil. Linseed oil loses its Omega 3 content when you heat it up. Take fried butter or coconut oil for frying and for everything else linseed oil. These fats you can digest well and they do not make you fat.

My Implementation:

Rule # 5: Avoid calcification, because lethally quiet trickles the calcification!

According to statistics, 80 to 90% of all elderly people suffer from calcification in some form. You have the best chance of being petrified like Lot's wife. Today, this does not happen suddenly, but much more "comfortable" on poles, walker, wheelchair, hospital bed. But it is still associated with hellish pain.

This is the future you will have when you are not getting active and helping your body wash out calcification and stop new deposits. Take lemon, apple vinegar, boron, K2, D3, magnesium! And move - daily!

My Implementation:

Rule # 6: Use the full power of Green Power!

We live in a very interesting time - which unfortunately holds loads of burdensome environmental influences and environmental toxins. Fire is best combated with fire, environmental toxins with environmental-natural-primal force. Prepare daily a green-power smoothie in which you mix in as much nature detoxification power as you can.

My Implementation:

Rule # 7: Use Essential Oils!

Believe me, there are pathogens behind every illness, really behind every illness. This applies to flu as well as rash, open legs, migraine, rheumatism, asthma, cardiovascular problems, MS, Parkinson's, cancer etc. etc.

The most effective weapon we have against it are essential oils. Only they combat reliably viruses, fungi, parasites, bacteria, prions. They have the great advantage that they cause no side effects and are also relatively cheap.

My Implementation:

Rule # 8: Free and regenerate your organs!

Plant mixtures help the organs to get rid of pollution. Plant power is the most efficient regeneration aid. If you want to avoid or get rid of countersinks, blockers, thinners, etc., then take care of your organs. Help them to regenerate with herbal blends and you will experience true, real wonders.

My Implementation:

Rule # 9: Use vital substances!

Healthy, powerful organs need vitamins, minerals, trace elements in harsh quantities. Analgesia, health and vitality up to the highest age is easily possible. Your organs will work as smoothly as you clean, care for, and give them enough natural vitality nutrients.

My Implementation:

_____

_____

_____

_____

_____

_____

_____

_____

_____

_____

_____

_____

_____

_____

_____

Rule # 10: Stay physically and mentally mobile!

Fitness is on everyone's lips. Most people understand this as only physical-athletic fitness. But it's about much more: Mental health. You can achieve this with a program that is as simple as it is effective: The Five Tibetans. They strengthen your immune system, keep you young, fit, physically and mentally alive.

My Implementation:

_____

_____

_____

_____

_____

_____

_____

_____

_____

_____

_____

_____

_____

Attachments

Number	Content
1	Omega 3, Omega 6
2	The acide-base balance
3	Enviromental pollution
4	Recipes for lime deposits
5	Sources of supply

Attachment 1: Approximate value (centent) Omega 3 : 6

Oils / Fat	Proportion Omega 3	Proportion Omega 6
Omega 3 excess fats / oils		
Linseed oil (flax oil)	56	15
Linseed	17	4
Chia seeds / oil	3	1
Fish	4 - 6	1
Omega 3 : 6 neutral fats / oils		
Butter	2	2
Cream	1	1
Frying butter	1	1
Coconut fat, organic quality	1	2
Omega 6 excess fats / oils		
Avocado, olives	0	2
Eggs, meat, chicken, dairy products	1	4 - 8
Rapeseed oil	9	26-55
Walnut	7	34
Olive oil, hempseed oil	1	8-15
Wheat germ oil	8	57
Nuts, except walnuts	1	7-35
Margarine	1	18-35
Pumpkin seed oil	1	54-100
Sunflower oil	1	66-140
Thistle oil	1	78-130
Evening primrose oil	1	80-100

The table shows it at a glance: Linseed oil is by far the omega 3 richest oil. Flax has been used since ancient times, flax is a human-friendly, native plant.

Attachment 2: The acid-base balance

Our organism does everything to maintain a balanced acid-base ratio. Unfortunately, that is not easy in our civilization. Far too many influences disturb the balance. In our everyday life, the acid clearly outweighs, so that acid-base is an issue that should be considered for a lifetime.

Most people have too much acid because

- our whole environment is sour,
- we have a lot of hectic, nervousness, excitement, stress, worries around us,
- we are exposed to mobile phones, WLAN, computers, photovoltaic, etc. rays. Rays, whose effects are not completely clear today [11]
- we usually eat more acidic foods than alkaline,
- many people have no idea what real acid bombs are, [12]
- we barely notice acid in everyday life. The organism excretes them from the blood, stores them in the tissue and tries to control them. This succeeds largely, until - yes, until the glass overflows once,
- conventional medicine does not provide a simple method for the determination of acid stored in the body, tissue or joints. Acid goes unnoticed for so long,
- the effectiveness of deacidification cures can hardly be controlled,

---

[11] Again and again one reads of whales swimming against the beach for no apparent reason and dying miserably. It is believed that the ship radio, that rays, disturbs the sense of orientation of whales. What negative effects our radiation-contaminated world has on us humans is not really known today.

[12] American specialist institutes such as Nutrition & Healing classifies white bread (= wheat = starch) plus fruit juices (= sugar) as the two most dangerous foods worldwide.

- hardly anyone can judge the quality of all the base remedies (salts, cures, herbs, etc.).

The German physician Hufeland [13] is credited with the following base recipe:
Heat 0.2 liters of water. Grate two medium-sized potatoes with a fine grater into the boiling water. Simmer for a few minutes. Eat the broth.

In the humoral medicine Kü-Ka-Lei-Wa is recommended:
- Bring 1 liter of water to a boil
- Add 1 tbsp caraway (seasoning)
- Wash well 500g of potatoes, do not peel,
- 2 tablespoons of flaxseed, not crushed,
- Simmer for 20 minutes, cook the potatoes properly, crush them
- Allow to cool and then strain
- Drink the whole liter during the day

Base powder
For many people, taking a base powder is easier. There are many in the market. In addition to minerals some also contain herbs or finely grated semi-precious stones. Mineral-containing healing clay is also available on the market.

---

[13] Christoph Wilhelm Hufeland, German physician, royal physician, 12.08.1976 - 25.08.1836. He is seen as the founder of macrobiotics.

Basically, the more different minerals are in the powder, the better it works: At least magnesium, selenium and zinc should be included, preferably also potassium.

Bases baths

Take pure, classic sea salt or a special base powder for full baths or foot baths: Duration 30 minutes.

If there is acidity (rheumatism, gout, joint pain) over a longer period of time, it makes sense to combine base powder / base baths with Hufeland or Kü-Ka-Lei-Wa.

Attachment 3: Enviromental pollution that can lead to diseases of all kinds

Our environment is full of pathogenic substances *

Chemicals we are exposed to:
- Pollution, industrial dust
- Cigarette, pipe, cigar smoke
- Car, bus, truck, aircraft exhaust
- Colours, solvents, adhesives: home-, office furniture: formaldehyde, toluene, benzene
- Toiletries: Cosmetics, hair spray, shampoo
- Vegetables, fruits, berries: Pesticides, herbicides, fungicides and chemical fertilizers

Heavy metals to which we are exposed:
- Tobacco smoke: Nickel, lead, cadmium, arsenic
- Cookware: Stainless steel, nickel, aluminum (and occasionally tin)
- Jewelry: (Cheap jewelry) Nickel (gold and silver are not endogenous metals)
- Hydrogenated fats and oils: Nickel
- Refined foods: Nickel
- Teeth: crowns: Amalgam, mercury (porcelain fillings: nickel)
- Fountain water: Lead, cadmium, aluminum

Electromagnetic fields to which we are exposed:
- Airplanes
- X-rays
- Sun in the high mountains
- Nuclear power plants
- LAN, WLAN
- Bluetooth

- Wireless phone
- Solar systems

ELF (low frequency) fields o which we are exposed:
- Microwave ovens
- Mobile phones, smart phones
- Electric heating pads
- Quartz watches
- Electric, electronic alarm clock
- Copper mattresses
- Water beds with heating
- TVs
- Lamps, energy-saving bulbs
- Computers, laptops, even if they are turned off
- Smoke detector

Foods that we eat:
- Hormones and antibiotics in the animal fattening
- Pesticides, fungicides, herbicides in cereals, vegetables, fruits, lettuce
- Preservatives, preservatives in food
- Toxic fats, trans fats
- Sugar and sugary foods
- Caffeine, caffeine-containing foods
- Processed and refined foods
- Alcohol
- Medicines

Synthetic fibers, synthetic materials, adhesives
In furniture, carpets, curtains, wallpaper, clothes
Materials such as clothes, bed linen, food products that have been
specially treated, e.g. with antiparasitic, antibacterial, antifungal
agents

* This list, these examples are from the book: "The Complete Cancer
Cleanse" by M.S. Cherie Calbom. Thomas Nelson Publishing, ISBN 978-
0-7852-8863-3

Attachment 4: Recipes against calcification deposits

Apple Cider Vinegar

Who has originally recommended apple cider vinegar, is hard to determine. Scientific studies on the application and effect are probably not available, but there are many enthusiastic reports.

Apple Cider Vinegar

- helps with arteriosclerosis,
- helps with diabetes (especially, to avoid the diabetes after-effects),
- lowers cholesterol,
- regulates digestion,
- has a filling effect, reduces ravenous appetite,
- lowers the blood sugar level,
- makes alkaline, regulates the acid-base balance,
- works against fungi and bacteria.

There are other voices that say apple cider vinegar helps

- to lose weight,
- gives a nice, firm skin,
- grooms the scalp, gives beautiful hair,
- Shall be a good wart remedy.

Application:

Apple cider vinegar is extremely easy to use: 1 tbsp. per 100 ml of water, fasting before eating.

Please only use pure, unpasteurized, naturally cloudy apple cider vinegar made from organic apples (apples only, no pears etc.)

Lemon drink by Dr. med. Johanna Budwig

How to prepare the drink:

- 1 liter of distilled or boiled water
- add the juice of 3 lemons (squeezed)
- add 1 piece of fresh grated ginger
- 3 teaspoons honey

Mix everything well by stirring. Keep the drink for one day at a temperature of 15 - 25 ° C. This achieves a slight maceration. Drink the whole liter the following day by glass. On the 2nd day set the liter for the 3rd day, on the 3rd day for the 4th etc. Always a week lemon drink, then a week break, then another week drink, etc.

This recipe is handed down from Dr. Johanna Budwig as a vitalizing drink. She writes:

The vitalizing drink strengthens the efficiency of the digestive organs. Poisonous deposits in the intestine are excreted and internal intestinal intoxication due to obstructed bowel movements is eliminated. Clogging, flatulence, rumors, indigestion, hard bowel movements and hemorrhoids are avoided. The lemon juice treatment helps to eliminate the chemical toxins that have taken root of parasites, fungi, yeast bacteria and intestinal bacteria. The immune system is thereby strengthened. This automatically increases our mental concentration and mental clarity. And there is a very popular side effect: Weight loss!

Attachment 5: Sources of supply

Chapter 6: Green Power
The most abundant green power concentrate currently (2018) may be: Orac-Energy Greens, by Paradise Greens, USA. Similarly, Macro Green Superfood from Macro Life Naturals, USA and All One Green Phyto Base from Nutritech, USA.

Chapter 7: Essential Oils
In many countries, essential oils are known only in the form of aroma therapy. A pity, because they can do a lot more. Search for essential oils that are packaged in capsules.
In Switzerland: Pharmacie des Eaux Vives, Geneva
In France: Search in the internet as well under «huiles essentielles»
In USA: Oregano Oil Intestinal Support contains oregano, ginger, fennel: NOW

Chapter 8 and 9: Vital substances, herbal regeneration aids
Any well-stocked pharmacy / drugstore can mix mother tincture drops and or spagyric mixtures. Many also have their own recipes ready. Pay attention to diversity, never use single substances, they can lead to dependencies.

Additional recommendations:

Topic	Product	Producer	Remarks
Multi-Vitamin	Orchard Plus und Garden Veggies	Natures Way, USA	Cost-effective, based on approximately 8 fruits and vegetables each. Identical / similar in many countries: Pinifit, Nutri Juice, Juice Plus.

	Vitalkomplex	Dr. Wolz, Germany	About 30 fruits, vegetables, herbs
	Miracle Reds Superfood	Macro Life Naturals, USA	The currently (2018) probably richest-containing multivitamin
	All One Original Formula	Nutritech, USA	Similar to Miracle Reds
	Alive Multivitamin	Natures Way, USA	Significantly richter than Orchard Plus, Garden Veggies
	Daily Vits	NOW, USA	Vitamins and minerals, good value for the money
	Eco Green	NOW, USA	Multivitamin with a large proportion of green
	Energy	NOW, US	Multivitamin with a high proportion of adaptogens (in case of stress)
	True Balance	NOW, USA	Helps liver and pancreas to better digest sugar and starch
Constipation	Super Colon Cleanse green	Health Plus, USA	Be sure to take the variant green
Liver, Gall	Liver Detox	Health Plus, USA	
Cardiovascular	Heart Support	Health Plus, USA	Magnesium, Pflants, Q10
	Natural Resveratrol 200mg	NOW, USA	Highly concentrated resveratrol

Veins	Leg & Veins	Natures Way, USA	Vitamin, Pflants, OPC
Respira-tory sys-tem	Lung, Bronchial & Sinus Health	Natural Fac-tors, USA	Plants
Urinary	Water Out	NOW, USA	Vitamin, minerals, plants
	Urinary	Natures Way, USA	Pflants
Spleen, Blood system	Blood Cleanse	Health Plus	Vitamins, minerals, plants
En-docrine system	Raw Multiple Glandular	Ultra Enter-prises, USA	Supports the hor-mon-producing or-gans
Nervous system	Nerve tonic	Liddel Lab, USA	Homeopatic remedie
	Relora	NOW, USA	Strengthen nervs
Structure Bones	Bone Strength	NOW, USA	Minerals, vitamins, boron
	Joint Cleanse	Health Plus, USA	Minerals, vitamins, collagen, plans
	Bone & Tissue Blend	Solaray,USA	Plants, mushrooms. To be completed with minerals
	Topfit	Phyto-pharma, CH	Minerals
	Collagen-Hyal-uronsäure-Drink	Natura Vita-lis, NL	Collagen, vege-tables, berries, vitamins

	UC II	NOW, USA	Collagen, Glucosamine, Chondroitin
	Boron	NOW, USA	Boron highly concentrated
	K 2	NOW, USA	Vitamin K, easy digestible
	Tri-3D Omega	NOW, USA	Omega 3 higly concentrated
	Glucosamine, Sulfate	Solaray, USA	Glucosamine, plants
Skin, hair	Hair & Skin	Natures Way, USA	Vitamins, healing plants
Eyes	Vision	Naures Way, USA	Vitamins, mienrals, healing plants

Zeitfracht Medien GmbH
Ferdinand-Jühlke-Straße 7
99095 Erfurt, Deutschland
produktsicherheit@kolibri360.de